MW01601858

David Darcy
A little help
for our friends

Published by David Darcy
www.mongrel.com.au

Text and photographs copyright © David Darcy 2009
First published in Australia 2009

ISBN 978-0-9806096-0-8

A CIP catalogue record for this publication is available from the National Library of Australia.

All rights reserved. No part of this publication may be reproduced, stored in a retrieval
system or transmitted in any form or by any means, electronic, mechanical, photocopying,
recording or otherwise, without the permission of the copyright holder.

Produced by Panographs Publishing Pty Ltd
Designed by Caz Brown based on a concept by David Darcy
Reprographics by CFL Print Studio
Printed in China by Everbest Printing Co. Ltd
Front cover: Daisy

Acknowledgements

Many thanks to John Lewis for support and encouragement over many years; Brett Wall for
your comradery and much-needed comedy during photographic adventures; Russel Bassett
and Miriam Rustemeyer for assistance beyond the boundary of true friendship; Rosie Vince,
'the unpaid secretary', for keeping the wheels on, on more than one occasion; Magnolia Flora
for editorial expertise during publication; Bayer Advantage for supporting this project;
George and Susan for the much needed helping hand; Mum and Gerd for dog sitting the
mongrels. And to all other family and friends, thank you.

Finally, to my wife Maria, who bears witness to my creative highs and lows, daily. Thank you
for stopping to smell the roses with me. Thank you for seeing the light, for holding strong and
staying true. But most of all thank you for allowing me to be me.

About *the book*

Since 1999, I've been chasing after dogs with a camera, in pursuit of a dream. My dream was to capture man's best friend at his leg lifting, butt sniffing, tail wagging best.

My inspiration for photographing dogs is borne from the bond I share with our four-legged friends, my passion for photography and a desire to portray dogs in a respectful manner (the way most of us know and remember our mates) without silly props and gimmicks.

My journey has taken me far and wide. From the dog next door to dingoes and working dogs in outback Australia; from mutts in Manhattan to canines in Cambodia; and hounds, pooches and mongrels in Tokyo, London and Hong Kong, I've witnessed a variety of happy dog moments.

A Little Help for Our Friends brings together some of my favourite photos of loved pets in Australia and around the world. It takes a look at life from the dogs' perspective. I hope it brings a smile to your face and reminds you of your best friend.

The blue barrow brothers

Don't let the droopy ears, the mudflap lips or the cute
button nose fool you, these guys are serious trouble makers.

playful

Holly

'Sixteen … 17 … 18 … 19 … 20 … coming ready or not!'

confident

Billy

'I've got the eyes of a hawk and the reflexes of a cat.
I just can't be bothered proving it.'

romantic

Lenny

'She's my world. I'd follow her to the end of the street.'

intuitive

Boof

'This can't be good. Mum's reaching for the dog shampoo.'

adventurous

cute

mischievous

devoted

peaceful

Chloe, Tyron, Bonnie, Huck, Charlie, Tess and Toby

Seven sleeping Labradoodles.

Following in our dads' pawprints

Born in a makeshift pen behind the tractor shed, working dogs begin their life on the land. Like their fathers, they'll chase sheep, ride in the ute, and sleep on the verandah in the late afternoon.

My friend

I know you're just a dog. People tell me that every day.
But you mean more to me than any anyone will ever know.

protective

Doc

'I'm in charge of the family heirlooms.
This one was Grandma's favourite.'

cheeky

Laughing larrikins

'Did you hear the one about the Irish Sheepdog?'

affectionate

Beanie and Nudge

'Hey Beanie, even though you beat me at rumbles today,
you're still my favourite sister.'

faithful

Home soon

'Sometimes the days are long, but knowing you'll
walk through the gate is all I need.'

charismatic

Jack

'Trust me, baby, you're the only one for me.'

Meet the mongrels

You won't find any pictures of blue-ribbon pooches in this family photo album. They're common old Bitsas and proud of it. Dad digs holes, Mum eats garbage and the kids all chase cats on the weekend.

alert

courageous

happy

eager

Days long gone

The paint on the walls is peeling and the timber floorboards are grey with age, but my memories of you haven't faded. I can still imagine you sitting at your favourite spot on the verandah.

sincere

Buddy

'Please don't ask me if your bum looks big in those jeans.'

tolerant

Lucy, Oscar and Tess

'This box is supposed to be for girls only.'

dependable

Jessie and Sam

'I listen to Jessie bark on and on, all day long, about sheep.
When I get home from work I like to kick back, forget
about sheep and just stare at the cat for a while.'

conscientious

Max

'It's just a power nap.'

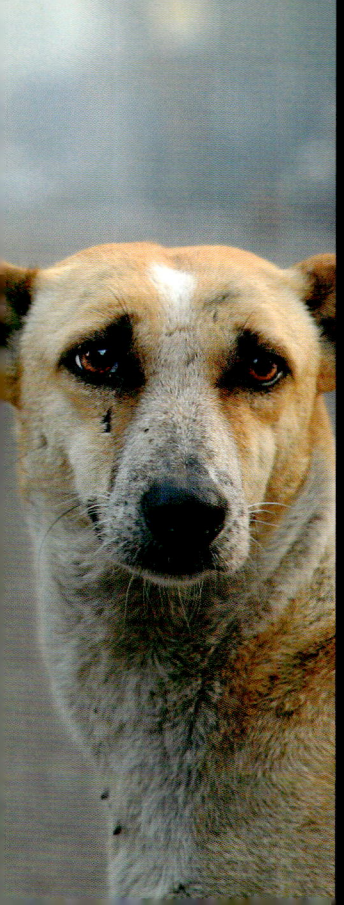

Friends in need

Dedication

In 2007, I embarked on my most significant photographic assignment to date – to document the field work of the volunteer veterinary organisation Vets Beyond Borders in India, which took me across boundaries both personal and professional. The assignment challenged my views, broke my heart and opened my eyes to a world that I knew very little about – the world of the street dog.

It is estimated that there are 400 million street dogs in the world. These dogs don't have a loving home, a bed or any veterinary care. Instead, they scratch out an existence amid danger, disease and urban waste. The problem is so big that it may seem beyond help, but we do have a chance to make a difference.

Non-government organisations such as
Vets Beyond Borders provide care for
the street dogs and education for local
communities. But they rely on charitable
donations and volunteers to undertake their
important work, which means they need
our support.

A Little Help for Our Friends was created to
remind us all of the wonderful relationship
we share with dogs. I hope it will also
encourage people to remember the plight of
the street dogs and inspire people everywhere
to help improve the lives of these dogs in
whatever way they can.

David Darcy
Sydney, 2009